W9-AQH-901

IMAGES
of America

ELLIS ISLAND

WITHDRAWN

*Dedicated to my colleagues in the
Museum Services Division at Ellis Island.*

IMAGES
of America

ELLIS ISLAND

Barry Moreno

ARCADIA

974.7
M843e
2008

CONTENTS

INTRODUCTION

Ellis Island appeals to anyone interested in America's rich immigrant heritage. In a quite remarkable way, it served as a sort of magnet in one of the greatest human migrations in the history of the world. In its day (a span of 62 years), it was the chief theater of the nation's immigration policies. Millions of aliens were detained there, if only briefly, and thousands were actually excluded and deported from there. We estimate that 12 million people passed through Ellis Island in its first 32 years of operation (1892 to 1924), and a few hundred thousand more passed through until its closure. Overall, nine-tenths of the foreigners who entered this country at Ellis Island were Europeans, and this bald fact reveals how significant it is to European history. Europe lost millions of its citizens and subjects to North America, an event that sundered family and kinship ties as well as political allegiances. In the early years of this mass migration, the U.S. government felt that it had a duty to regulate the flow through Ellis Island and other stations by keeping out unwelcome strangers. The most common of these were the diseased and sickly, the criminally inclined or immoral, and those whom politicians feared might become charity cases. The newcomers were welcome to these shores so long as they represented a vibrant fresh workforce to fuel the nation's industries and businesses. Thus, most American immigration laws until 1917 were relatively permissive. Only as the immigration numbers rose precipitously after the turn of the century did Congress begin seriously debating immigration restriction. Between 1914 and 1918, immigration dropped severely due to the war in Europe. The change showed that America's industries could do without the constant flow of fresh "greenhorns" off the ships. This inspired critics to press for severe cuts in immigration. The new pressure finally compelled Congress to enact stiff quota laws in 1921 and 1924 that cut immigration to a mere trickle by the end of the decade. It was generally agreed that immigration was no longer in the national interest. From that time forward, Ellis Island was no longer the golden door to North America. It then served as the nation's top detention and deportation station until the last alien left the island on November 12, 1954.

A brief explanation of the immigration procedures may help the reader understand what went on at Ellis Island. Emigrants bought their steamship tickets and supplied all their personal information for the ship's manifest to the ticketing agent in the old country or the port of departure. They underwent medical examinations and vaccinations at most ports of departure and once again when aboard the steamship on the high seas. Prior to 1920, there was no nonsense about passports or visas since they were not needed to enter the United States. On arrival in New York harbor, steamships slowly proceeded to their piers in Manhattan, Brooklyn, or Hoboken, and steerage and third-class passengers—the immigrants—were brought to Ellis Island via barges for inspection. Cabin passengers, who were not regarded as immigrants, were processed aboard ship; only a few were detained and taken to Ellis Island.

At Ellis Island, immigrants underwent line inspection by U.S. Public Health Service physicians. The first doctor, called an "eye man," carefully lifted eyelids. He was looking for signs of faulty vision and diseases like trachoma, conjunctivitis, and cataracts. Of these, trachoma was the most feared, since certifying this disease gave the immigration inspectors in the registry room no alternative but to send the alien back to his country of origin. Millions in North Africa, especially children, still suffer from trachoma today. A second doctor checked for general physical and mental fitness and acceptable hygiene. This second part of the line inspection was known as the "medical gaze," because the doctors could supposedly discover any sign of illness by simply watching an immigrant for 6 to 40 seconds. After safely passing these probing doctors, immigrants mounted the staircase to the registry room. Here, an inspector made the decision to admit, reject, or detain an alien. The questions he put to each immigrant were drawn from responses already recorded on the steamship's manifest, and additional questions were asked when complications arose. Since most foreigners spoke no English, an interpreter provided translations. An inspector carefully listened to and watched each immigrant for any sign of inadmissibility. Problem cases or suspicious aliens were detained temporarily or for special inquiry, hospitalization, or exclusion. Most aliens had no trouble passing through these bureaucratic steps and were released after about five hours. They went down the stairs of separation and made for either the Ellis Island ferryboat bound for Manhattan or to the railroad dock behind the main building to take a boat to the train station in Jersey City. After leaving Ellis Island, most were out of New York and New Jersey within hours and were on their way to any number of destinations in the United States and Canada.

The pictures in this book are like paintings mounted in golden frames; they give the modern eye a wonderful glimpse of mankind's struggle in the changing world of 1890 through 1950. They tell the stories of millions of people who still lived only at the verge of modernity and whose knowledge of America came to them in bits and pieces. Much of what they knew about it was derived by word of mouth or from a letter, booklet, or even silent film—all quite faulty methods for researching so great a journey. This book spans more than a century and tells not only the immigrants' story but also the story of various federal government agencies and their bureaucrats at Ellis Island over the years, including the U.S. Bureau of Immigration, the Coast Guard, the U.S. Public Health Service, and the National Park Service. This book pays tribute to them all.

—Barry Moreno
Staten Island
July 2003

One

FROM CASTLE GARDEN TO ELLIS ISLAND

IN AN ENGLISH PORT. Pictured here is a common boarding scene of emigrants as they prepare for their long journey over the seas in the 1800s. To the right, a man is handing out dolls to a crowd of girls; in the center, a matron tries to console a young woman; behind them, more passengers bearing boxes board the ship.

CASTLE GARDEN. This was America's first immigrant station. Opened in August 1855, it was operated by the government of New York State and became a symbol to European emigrants. By the time it closed in April 1890, some eight million immigrants had passed through its halls. Its top immigrant groups were the Germans, Scandinavians, Irish, English, Scottish, and French. Many became homesteaders in the Midwest or Canada.

A CLOSER LOOK AT CASTLE GARDEN. Located at the southern tip of Manhattan, Castle Garden was in an ideal location for ships' captains to send their foreign passengers for immigration inspection. This c. 1888 view shows the numerous buildings within the complex, such as the infirmary and the intelligence office. The Statue of Liberty can be seen in the distance. A series of scandals eventually forced the station to be closed.

AT THE CASTLE GARDEN LABOR EXCHANGE, THE 1860S. This telling sketch shows a crowd of immigrants looking for work. A Scotsman (left) is standing in front of a German trunk. The others are mainly Germans. All appear calm and have not noticed that a robber (right) is rifling through a woman's purse.

THE OCEAN CROSSING. Joseph Byron snapped this shot of immigrant passengers taking the sun and air on the steerage deck of the steamship *Pennland* in 1890.

GOOD HUMOR AT SEA. Here, Joseph Byron caught a cheerful moment in the lives of these emigrant passengers of the *Pennland*. In spite of the sunlight, it is clearly a chilly day on deck.

A GLIMPSE OF THE HEAVENS. In this 1890 view from the *Pennland*, an immigrant serenely takes a skyward glance as her fellow travelers scowl at the cameraman.

ELLIS ISLAND. Before the Europeans came, the local Native Americans called it Gull Island, or *kioshk*. There they gathered oysters, clams, and mussels and fished for striped bass and flounder. The Dutch bought the island from the Native Americans in 1630 and named it Little Oyster Island. In 1774, Samuel Ellis (1712–1794) purchased it. The federal government gained ownership of the island in 1808 and built Fort Gibson there, as seen in this drawing.

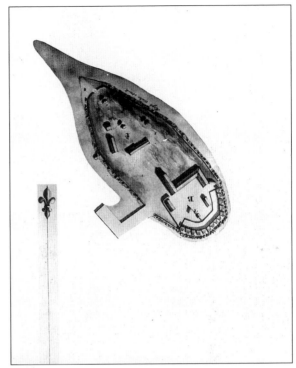

HORSES, WAGONS, AND IMMIGRANTS AT THE BARGE OFFICE. In 1890, Congress and President Harrison chose Ellis Island as the site of the first federally operated immigrant receiving station. While the new station was being built, the government used the barge office, pictured here, as a temporary landing place for immigrants. It was located at the edge of Battery Park and within sight of Castle Garden.

COL. JOHN B. WEBER, COMMISSIONER OF ELLIS ISLAND, 1890–1893. A busy man, Weber ran the barge office, oversaw the construction work on Ellis Island, investigated emigration conditions in Europe, and opened Ellis Island in 1892. John Baptiste Weber (1842–1926) commanded an African American regiment during the Civil War. In the 1880s, he was the congressman for Buffalo and Lackawanna and ended his career as commissioner of the Pan-American Exposition of 1901.

REGISTRY INSPECTORS. This barge office photograph shows the first federal registry inspectors, who were paid $1,200 annually, all of whom had worked previously at Castle Garden and would continue on at Ellis Island. Seen here are, from left to right, the following: (seated) Najeeb J. Arbeely, M.N. Gilbertson, D.T. Van Duzer, and R.W. Conradson; (standing) Christian A. Raven, S.A. Smith, and Charles Semsey. Arbeely, a Syrian immigrant, was fluent in Arabic and French.

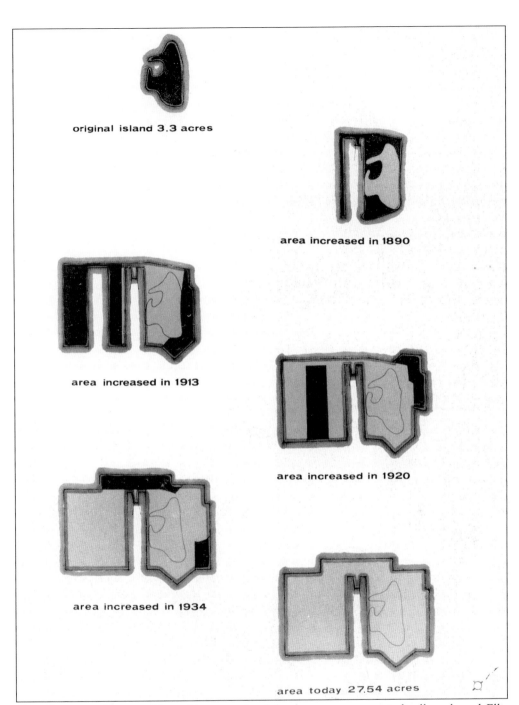

original island 3.3 acres

area increased in 1890

area increased in 1913

area increased in 1920

area increased in 1934

area today 27.54 acres

THE GROWING ISLAND. Over the years, the federal government periodically enlarged Ellis Island through landfill operations. The pressing need for more buildings finally resulted in the island's present size of 27.54 acres. Under a 1997 Supreme Court ruling, the landfilled areas are part of New Jersey, and the original island remains within the state of New York.

THE FIRST STATION AT ELLIS ISLAND, 1892–1897. Designed by J. Bachmeyer of the U.S. Public Buildings Service and constructed in 1891 by Sheridan and Byrne, the new station, made of Georgia pine, had buff-painted walls and a blue slate roof. *Harper's Weekly* declared that it resembled a "latter-day watering place hotel." It was destroyed in a terrific fire on the morning of June 15, 1897.

THE FIRST IMMIGRANT. Irish immigrant Annie Moore, who traveled to the United States aboard the *Nevada*, received a surprise when she arrived at Ellis Island on January 1, 1892, since she was the first to land at the newly built station. Commissioner Weber gave her a $10 gold piece, and a Catholic priest gave her a blessing. Charles M. Hendley registered her and her brothers and then turned them over to their father, Matthew Moore.

ANNIE'S GOLDEN GREETING

The First Immigrant to Land on Ellis Island Got $10.

SHE WAS A LITTLE IRISH GIRL COME TO JOIN HER PARENTS.

The New Landing Station Was Formally Opened Yesterday by Col. Weber. Everything Worked Smoothly, and the Provisions for the Care and Comfort of the Immigrants Are Generally Praised—Little Annie's Welcome.

Annie Moore is the name of a little girl who who was born in the city of Cork, Ireland, fifteen years ago yesterday.

Her father, Matt Moore, lives at No. 32 Monroe street, in this city.

ANNIE MOORE O'CONNELL (1877–1923). After living in Manhattan, the family moved to Indiana and then to Texas. Pictured *c.* 1906 is Annie Moore with her infant daughter Mary Catherine O'Connell. The couple had six children before O'Connell's death, which left Annie a struggling widow. Tragically, she was killed in a train accident in 1923.

17

AN IMMIGRANT INSPECTION. André Castaigne drew this marvelous sketch of an inspector, helped by an interpreter, registering an alien in 1896. The building in which this inspection took place was burned to the ground in 1897.

MAIN BUILDING
FRONT ELEVATION

U.S. IMMIGRANT STATION

ELLIS ISLAND

SCALE ⅛INCH = 1 FOOT

MAIN BUILDING
Drawing, DT N° 4.
Boring and Tilton
ARCHITECTS

THE DESIGN FOR THE NEW MAIN BUILDING. This is the approved design for the main building of the second immigrant receiving station at Ellis Island. The fireproof structure is built of limestone and an arrangement of bricks laid in Flemish bond upon a framework of steel. The general style is that of the French Renaissance. The building was designed by the architects William Boring and Edward Tilton in 1897–1898. This blueprint includes the required signatures of James Knox Taylor, supervisory architect for the Department of the Treasury, and three cabinet secretaries, including Secretary of the Interior Cornelius Bliss, who had been a prominent fundraiser for the Statue of Liberty in the 1880s.

AN AMERICAN EMBLEM EMBEDDED IN STONE. One of the stunning architectural features at the entrance to the main building is a pair of ornamental bald eagles perched atop escutcheons of the Stars and Stripes. Such ornamentation was quite suited to the building's Beaux-Arts style. For the building's design, Boring and Tilton were awarded the gold medal at the Paris Exhibition of 1900.

BUILDING THE NEW SEA WALL. The Phoenix Construction Company began building a concrete- and granite-faced sea wall on the north side of the ferry basin, as seen in this August 1913 photograph.

AN AERIAL VIEW OF ELLIS ISLAND. Dating from *c.* 1920, this picture shows the immaculate landscape of Island One, where the main building is located, while in the foreground, the space between Islands Two and Three have yet to be filled in completely. Most of the landfilling for this area took place between 1924 and 1932.

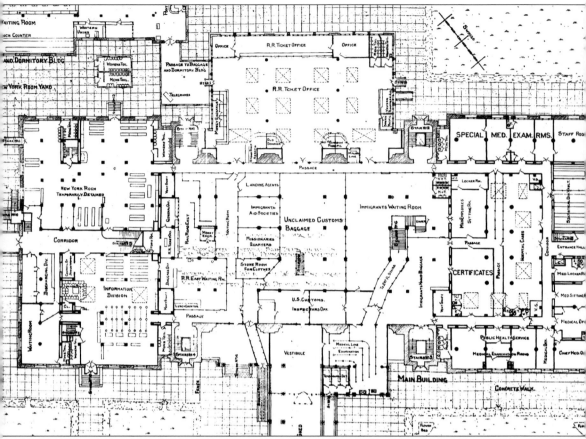

A Plan of the Ground Floor of the Main Building, 1907. This remarkable diagram reveals the complexity of immigration control at America's greatest station during its busiest year ever. In 1907, some 1,285,000 people were tabulated at the island. The central area shows the customs inspectors' office, the medical examinations lines, the immigrants' hand baggage storage area, and separate rooms for the missionaries, immigrant aid societies, and steamship landing agents. The right wing of the building is given over to the U.S. Public Health Service, and the left wing includes a large room for temporarily detained aliens bound for New York, the information division, the discharging division, and a private room for the National Council of Jewish Women.

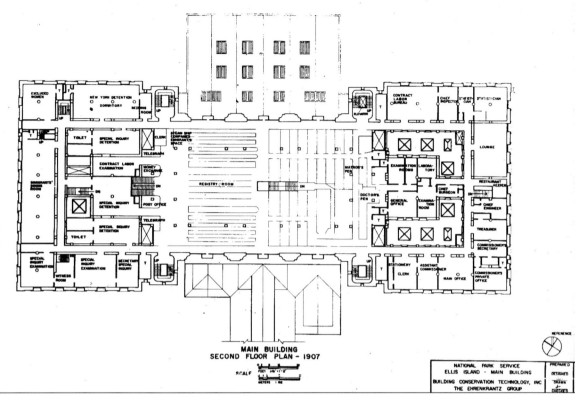

MAIN BUILDING
SECOND FLOOR PLAN - 1907

SCALE

NATIONAL PARK SERVICE	PREPARED
ELLIS ISLAND - MAIN BUILDING	DESIGNED
BUILDING CONSERVATION TECHNOLOGY, INC	DRAWN
THE EHRENKRANTZ GROUP	CHECKED

A PLAN OF THE SECOND FLOOR OF THE MAIN BUILDING, 1907. This drawing shows us how the second level was disposed. In the middle of the registry room (Great Hall) was a central staircase that led the immigrants into an alleyway of iron pens. These were like cattle pens, and some immigration employees jokingly called their foreign charges animals. As can be seen, doctors had special pens wherein to detain those suspected of illness, and matrons had pens for women requiring care or under suspicion. The right wing of this floor was primarily devoted to the U.S. Bureau of Immigration and included the commissioner's private office, the contract labor bureau, and the medical examination areas, including the "mental room." The left wing was given over to detention. It housed the special inquiry division, including two hearing rooms, detention rooms, a witness room, the New York detention dormitory, the immigrants' dining room, and the excluded women's room.

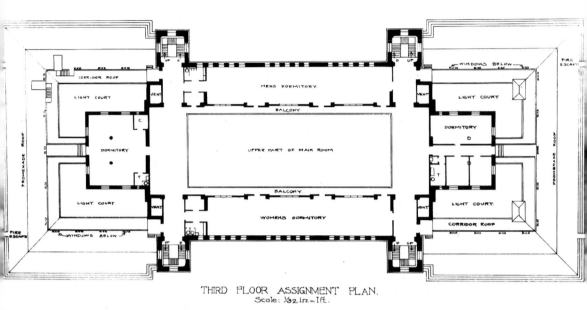

THIRD FLOOR ASSIGNMENT PLAN.
Scale: 1/32 in.=1ft.

MAIN BUILDING

A PLAN OF THE THIRD FLOOR OF THE MAIN BUILDING, 1907. This simple layout shows the balcony level and the respective male and female dormitories on opposite sides. The right and left wings contain two more dormitories as well as light courts and promenades where exercise and a breath of fresh air could be had.

Two

YEARS OF GLORY, YEARS OF CONTROVERSY

THE COMMISSIONER-GENERAL WITH THE ELLIS ISLAND STAFF. This 1906 photograph was taken to commemorate the official visit of Frank Sargent, commissioner-general of immigration, who had come up from Washington, D.C. The mustachioed commissioner-general stands in the front on the lower step on the right, while on the opposite side, Robert Watchorn, commissioner of Ellis Island, stands behind two women. Those photographed are primarily division chiefs, hand-picked inspectors, interpreters, and matrons. Interestingly, a black inspector can be seen in the very rear on the right-hand side. Sargent (1854–1908) kept a close watch on events at Ellis Island and was supportive of his commissioners there, William Williams (1902–1905) and Robert Watchorn (1905–1909).

COMMISSIONER ROBERT WATCHORN WITH VISITING DIGNITARIES. This splendidly Edwardian picture shows a hatless Commissioner Watchorn standing on the Ellis Island boardwalk with his guests. The photograph was taken by chief clerk Augustus F. Sherman. Robert Watchorn (1858–1944) was a native of Derbyshire, England, and had emigrated to the United States in the early 1870s. He worked in the coal mines of Pennsylvania but through striving and ambition worked his way into an important position in his trade union. After serving as secretary to the governor of Pennsylvania, he entered the U.S. Bureau of Immigration and worked as an inspector at Ellis Island. He was promoted to the post of commissioner at the Montreal station, and in 1905, Pres. Theodore Roosevelt named him as successor at Ellis Island to the brilliant commissioner William Williams (1862–1947). After serving at Ellis Island, Watchorn resigned from the government and launched a successful career as an oil executive.

APPLYING FOR EMIGRATION DOCUMENTS IN POLAND. This picture, taken at Warsaw, gives some idea of the great masses of Jews who were flocking to get out of eastern Europe. In this scene, the people are applying for emigration documents. More than one and a half million Jews immigrated through Ellis Island.

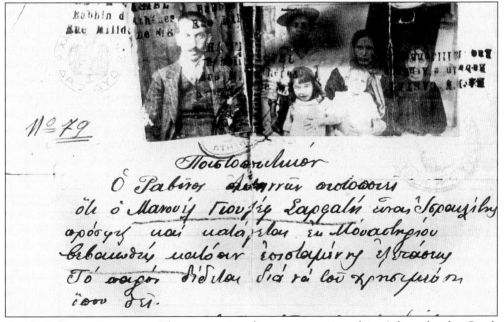

A 1916 GREEK PASSPORT. This interesting document was issued in Athens by the Greek government to a Jewish rabbi and his family.

Cⁱᵉ Gᵉˡᵉ TRANSATLANTIQUE
FRENCH LINE

Paquebot "Paris"

HAVRE — NEW YORK

A EUROPEAN STEAMSHIP ADVERTISEMENT. This is a classic advertisement of one of Europe's great steamship companies, the Compagnie Générale Translatlantique, better known to Americans as the French Line. The *Paris*, which was on the Le Havre–New York service, was one of the great ocean liners of the era. Aside from French emigrants, this line also attracted Belgians, Luxembourgers, the Swiss, Austrians, Armenians, and Russians.

INSPECTION CARD

(Immigrants and Steerage Passengers).

The East-Asiatic Company, Limited.
BALTIC AMERICA LINE.

Port of departure, DANZIG.   S. S. Estonia

Name of ship,

Name of Immigrant,   Izacki, Izer

Date of departure,

Last residence,   Poland

Inspected and passed ad DANZIG.	Passed at quarantine, port of	Passed by Immigration Bureau
UNITED STATES PUBLIC HEALTH SERVICE Seal Stamp by Consul or Medical Officer	SENT TO HOSPITAL DEC 4 1925 (Date).	port of (Date).

(The following to be filled in by ship's surgeon or agent prior to or after embarkation).

Ship's list or manifest   10   No. on ship's list or manifest   17

Berth No.	Steamship inspection	1st day	1	2	3	4	5	6	7	8	9	10	11	12	13	14	15	16	17	18	19

No. 37c. 5000. 5. 24.

A MEDICAL INSPECTION CARD. During the sea voyage to America, emigrants were supposed to receive several medical examinations. This medical inspection card shows that Izek Izacki, a passenger aboard the Baltic America Line's steamer *Estonia*, sailing out of the port of Danzig (Gdansk), was hospitalized directly upon his arrival at Ellis Island.

A Red Star Line Steerage Deck. In this 1901 photograph, a crowd of weary immigrants tries to relax and get a breath of fresh air on the steerage deck of the Belgian steamer *Westernland*. Unpleasant neighbors, awful stenches, and cramped conditions were common for passengers in steerage quarters below. Such a voyage could take anywhere from five days to five weeks.

THE HUDDLED MASSES AT SEA. Here is a typical scene taken aboard the steerage deck of a transatlantic steamer. The wonderful thing about the picture is the cooperation of the passengers with the cameraman.

THE DOCKING OF THE ADRIATIC. Immigrants are preparing to be disembarked from the steerage deck of this White Star Line vessel. The picture was taken on July 2, 1923.

PREPARING TO LAND IN AMERICA. Their voyage at an end, these immigrants are busily preparing for disembarkation.

BAGS AND BAGGAGE. Here, the steerage passengers are surrounded by their many and varied possessions, all of which would have to be checked by the federal customs inspectors before they could be processed at Ellis Island.

ABOARD THE BREMEN. Here, a crowd of Germans is photographed aboard a North German Lloyd steamship in 1925. About 600,000 Germans passed through Ellis Island.

YOUNG EDWARD FLANAGAN COMES TO AMERICA. Edward Joseph Flanagan (1886–1948), the big fellow in the front, is seen here with his brother Patrick and fellow Irish passengers aboard the *Celtic*. The ship docked in New York harbor on August 27, 1904. Both Flanagans were eventually ordained as priests. Edward Flanagan founded Boys Town in Nebraska and was one of the Catholic Church's great reformers of juveniles.

ONE OF THE 1,000 MARRIAGEABLE GIRLS. This engaging picture of one of the "thousand marriageable" girls aboard the White Star steamship *Baltic* in 1907 brings in clear focus the rising numbers of female immigrants who set out for America in search of husbands. This young woman is either English or Irish. Slightly more than one million immigrants from Great Britain and Ireland passed through Ellis Island.

A GOVERNMENT WELCOME. On entering the port of New York, steamships were met by the U.S. Bureau of Immigration's cutter that carried boarding inspectors, a clerk, a doctor, and often a matron. Their task was to ascertain information on all foreign passengers, obtain the ship's manifest, question all cabin-class passengers, possibly detaining a few, and tag all steerage and third-class passengers and deliver them safely to Ellis Island for inspection.

FROM NEW JERSEY TO ELLIS ISLAND. After undergoing customs inspection in Hoboken, New Jersey, passengers from German or Dutch steamers were put aboard a barge and ferried over to Ellis Island. Until the 1920s, Hoboken was one of the most German cities on the eastern seaboard.

ELLIS ISLAND AND MANHATTAN FROM THE AIR. This c. 1931 photograph shows the landfilling on Ellis Island to be just about complete.

THE MAIN BUILDING WITH CANOPY. Pictured here is the main building *c.* 1905. The stillness of the image, taken early in the morning, gives a majestic, serene air to the place before the restless crowds of immigrants and immigration staff cluttered its walkways and halls.

THE IMMIGRATION CUTTER AT ELLIS ISLAND. This splendid photograph provides a close view of the boarding division's cutter, which took inspectors and other staff members from the barge office in the Battery to the steamships in the harbor every morning and afternoon. To its rear is a ferry that brought immigrants to Ellis Island from the New York and New Jersey piers.

A CROWD OF IMMIGRANTS. This is one of chief clerk Augustus Sherman's photographs. The men in the rear are Italians.

THE EYE MEN. One of the dreaded annoyances for arriving immigrants was to have to undergo the eye examination. This examination was carried out by U.S. Public Health Service surgeons who everted immigrants' eyelids in search of any sign of the dangerous contagious disease trachoma.

A Closeup View of the Eye Examination. Trachoma was not the only visual disorder that the doctors were on the watch for. They also looked for the signs of conjunctivitis. All suspects of eye disease were chalk-marked with the letters "E" or "Ct" (trachoma) and were temporarily locked in a cage with other medical detainees. When line inspection was completed, the doctors took the whole group away to the examination rooms.

Medical Inspection in the Great Hall. The eye examination received a good deal of comment in the press during the first two decades of the 20th century. This picture shows the fencing system, or pens, on the second floor through which immigrants moved during immigrant inspection.

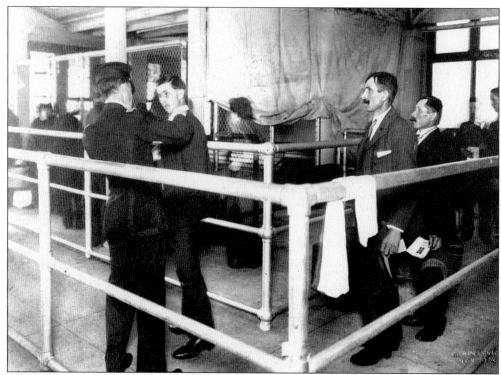

PHYSICAL EXAMINATION. Another set of doctors gave immigrants the "six-second physical," quickly scanning for signs of physical or mental illness. The merest suspicion would cause a doctor to take out his piece of chalk and write a mark on an immigrant's coat. For example, "B" stood for back, "Ft" for feet, "H" for heart, "K" for hernia, "S" for senility, and "X" for feeble-mindedness.

THE IMMIGRATION LINE IN THE REGISTRY ROOM. This 1907 photograph gives an idea of the rising tide of women who immigrated to the United States after 1900. Women unescorted by a male relative were either temporarily detained or excluded altogether.

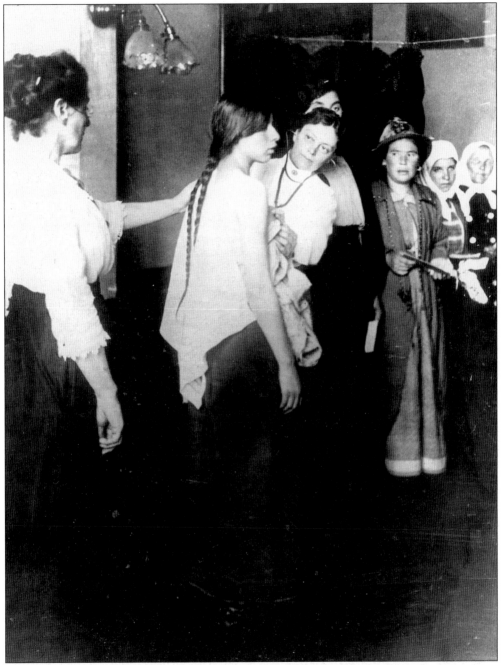

THE DOCTOR IS A WOMAN. In 1914, Dr. Rose A. Bebb was appointed the first woman physician at Ellis Island. This made gynecological examinations for signs of pregnancy or disease more endurable for female immigrants.

IN THE MENTAL ROOM. A detained "mental suspect" was brought into this room and sat on a row of benches with other suspects until his turn came to walk up to this desk and try to put together the wooden puzzles and answer a series of questions. Of 40 people examined, only one or two might be certified as feeble-minded and returned to his country of origin.

THE MAIN HOSPITAL BUILDINGS. Standing directly across the ferry slip from the main building, the immigrant hospital on the right was completed in 1901, and the hospital extension on the left was added in 1905. The U.S. Public Health Service's administrative offices were located in the middle building. Too far to the right to be seen in this photograph is the psychopathic ward, which was added in November 1907.

CARING FOR THE SICK. This Ellis Island nurse (rear) is shown with an Asian immigrant family in the early 1920s. The Chinese were the largest Asian nationality to pass through Ellis Island.

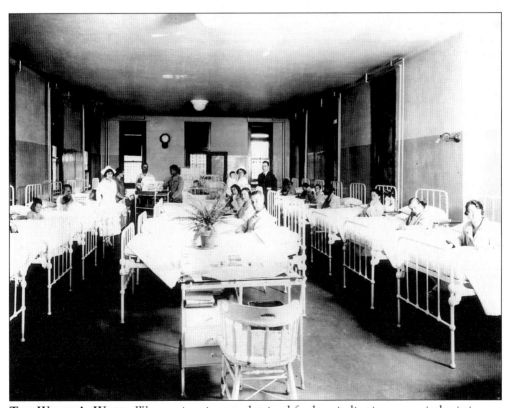

THE WOMEN'S WARD. Women immigrants detained for hospitalization are quietly sitting on chairs next to their freshly made beds in this arranged photograph.

THE REGISTRY ROOM, 1903. This magnificent picture gives a sense of the arrangement of the Great Hall 100 years ago. The camera faces the great system of pens and alleyways leading to the registry inspectors' desks, where the interrogations took place, and the stairs of separation at the end. As can be seen here, the immigrants were expected to stand in line during the entire procedure.

NATIONAL IMMIGRATION DELEGATES VISIT ELLIS ISLAND. Americans and foreigners were fascinated by events at Ellis Island, and a constant stream of visitors came out to the island to witness the examinations of thousands of foreigners. Distinguished visitors included Italy's Duke of the Abruzzi, the celebrated novelists Henry James and H.G. Wells, and American presidents Theodore Roosevelt, William Howard Taft, and Woodrow Wilson.

THE IMMIGRANT PENS. This is a splendid view of the complex system that kept the immigrant crowds under control from 1900 through 1911. Criticized by many as insulting and inhumane, the system was removed in the latter year and replaced by rows of wooden benches.

THE WOODEN BENCH ROW SYSTEM. When the pens were removed in 1911, they were replaced by these rows of wooden benches. Many have survived and are currently on display at Ellis Island.

AN IMMIGRANT FAMILY. Women and children were detained until an adult male relative could come for them.

TAGGED ALIENS. This mother and son in thick coats still have their steamship manifest tags on. The photograph was taken by Augustus Sherman.

A MOTHER AND CHILDREN. This is a typical scene in the registry and waiting rooms.

AN ITALIAN MOTHER AND CHILDREN. This photograph was taken in the registry room in the first decade of the 20th century.

AT THE REGISTRY INSPECTORS' DESKS. The men on the left decided the fate of immigrants. They had to determine whether an alien had to be barred or allowed to land. The hatless mustachioed official looking directly into the camera is Peter Mikolainis, a Lithuanian interpreter, who knew several other languages as well. Mikolainis (1868–1934) was himself an immigrant, having come to the United States in the 1890s. Employed at Ellis Island from 1903 to 1913, he strove in every way possible to help his fellow Lithuanians.

THE INSPECTOR SPEAKS. This woman has on her dress a series of chalk marks that she received during her medical examination. The first two are "K" for hernia and "B" for back. The inspector questioning her is holding her steamship papers. Females and immigrant children who were traveling without an adult male relative and had none to meet them at Ellis Island often faced the prospect of temporary detention or exclusion.

AN INTERPRETER AND AN ALIEN. This 1926 photograph shows a white-haired inspector carefully making notes while an interpreter (center) questions an alien in a foreign language. Thirty-six foreign languages were translated at Ellis Island by inspectors, matrons, guards, medical personnel, charwomen, and the official interpreters themselves.

IN THE BAGGAGE ROOM. This boy and girl stand with one of their possessions in the baggage room on the first floor.

WAITING. Two Arab women clutch their papers in their hands and tensely sit through yet another stage of the immigration process.

A FINNISH STOWAWAY. This detained stowaway was photographed at Ellis Island in 1926. Stowaways were sent to the special inquiry division for judgment. Many were found admissible.

A BOARD OF SPECIAL INQUIRY HEARING. Three inspectors determined problem cases sent to them by the registry division, including immigrants certified with a excludable disease, stowaways, criminals, and all complicated situations. The boards also handled appeal cases.

A SPECIAL INQUIRY CASE. The tension in this room is clearly evident. Working at Ellis Island in a decision-making capacity could be emotionally draining, especially given the long working hours and the six-day workweek.

AN APPEAL TO THE COMMISSIONER. Commissioner Robert Watchorn (holding papers) listens intently while an inspector explains the case of the two immigrants who stand in silence. Chief clerk Augustus F. Sherman is seated on the right.

THE MONEY EXCHANGE. Having at last passed through immigration inspection, the new arrivals were now landed and free to prepare to leave Ellis Island for their various destinations. Before leaving, however, most changed their foreign money for dollars. The sign announcing the money exchange in English includes translations in Italian, German, French, Swedish, Hungarian, and Polish. The American Express Company operated the money exchange for nearly 50 years.

THE RAILROAD ROOM. In this area of the main building's ground floor, immigrants could buy train tickets from agents representing such firms as the New York Central Railroad, the Union Pacific Railroad, and the Rock Island line.

THE LUNCH COUNTER. Here, immigrants could buy a large boxed lunch for $1 or a small one for 50¢. The packages contained various selections of roast beef, ham, or kosher bologna sandwiches and sardines, sweet cakes, pies, oranges, and apples. Beverages, including milk, tea, coffee, and sweet cider, were also sold.

FREE TO LAND. Once through the various hurdles arranged for them at Ellis Island, the immigrants now might only guess what lay ahead.

THE IMMIGRANT TRAIN. These men have cleared inspection at Ellis Island. Exhausted, they sleep in a railway carriage. This is probably the special immigrant train that departed at 9:00 p.m. from the Jersey City terminal.

Three
AN ALBUM OF NATIONS

PASSENGERS FROM THE *PRETORIA*. Herr and Frau Jakob Mithelstadt, with their daughter and seven sons, were among the thousands of Germans who abandoned their homes in Russia to make the journey to America. This picture was taken at Ellis Island on May 9, 1905. Their destination was Kuln, North Dakota. Most Germans from Russia became homesteaders. The photograph was taken by Augustus Sherman.

A WOMAN OF HOLLAND. In this Augustus Sherman photograph, a Dutch immigrant wears the folk costume typical of her native Zeeland.

A BAMBINO ARRIVES. This hardy young Italian lad in a hooded cape lugged his own box on what must have been a cold day at Ellis Island in 1926. He probably traveled with his mother or another female relative. Italian women with children usually came to join their husbands in the vibrant world of America's many Little Italys.

A HUNGARIAN MOTHER AND CHILD.
This young woman is one of 350,000
Hungarians who entered the United States
through Ellis Island. They were
photographed on January 17, 1925.

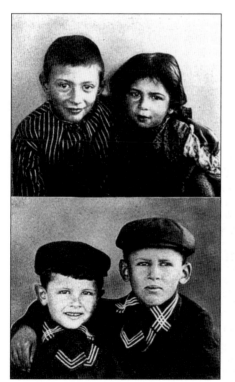

A QUARTET FROM PORTUGAL AND SPAIN. Above
are a Portuguese boy and girl, and below are two
Spanish boys at Ellis Island. The photographs date
from *c.* 1905. About 120,000 Portuguese and
70,000 Spanish immigrants passed through Ellis
Island. Many of the Portuguese were from Madeira
and the Cape Verde Islands, as well as from the
mainland. Famous Spanish immigrants include
silent-film star Antonio Moreno and the Catalan-
born musician Xavier Cugat.

THREE SCOTS IN KILTS. These three children, dressed in their national costumes, arrived at Ellis Island on Armistice Day 1920 as passengers of the *Columbia*. Augustus Sherman took this photograph. Famous Scottish immigrants include the legendary actor Donald Crisp, as well as trade union leaders Philip Murray and Douglas Fraser, journalist James Reston, and jazz singer Annie Ross.

CHILDREN OF THE NETHERLANDS. The Dutch were a favorite with Augustus Sherman, who found them quite photogenic.

A Czech Grandmother.
Relatives probably sent for this woman to come and join them in America. More than 100,000 Czechs—then labeled either Bohemian or Moravian—were processed at Ellis Island.

A Wealthy Dane in Search of Pleasure. This is how Augustus Sherman titled this photograph of Peter Meyer, who arrived c. 1910. Some 90,000 Danes immigrated through Ellis Island. Most of them settled in Midwest states such as Iowa, Nebraska, and Minnesota.

AN ENGLISH JEWISH FAMILY. This charmingly dressed family was photographed by Augustus Sherman. Notable English-born Jews to pass through Ellis Island include New York City mayor Abraham Beame and vaudeville comic Henny Youngman.

A YOUNG HINDU. This immigrant was one of a thousand or so Indians who passed through Ellis Island. He had sailed from England in 1911 aboard a White Star Line vessel.

YUGOSLAVS AT ELLIS ISLAND. These Yugoslavs arrived in June 1924. While in detention, they were aided by Ludmila K. Foxlee, a prominent social-service worker of the YWCA.

A CROWD FROM GUADELOUPE. These 24 women were in transit to Montreal to take up work as household servants. They were passengers from the steamship *Korona*, which arrived in the port of New York on April 6, 1911. In the upper right-hand corner of this Augustus Sherman photograph stands an unidentified man.

THE ITALIAN PIPER. At 37 years old, Antonio Piestineola had just come off the *San Giovanni* when he agreed to pose for Augustus Sherman on May 17, 1908. He is playing a most curious type of bagpipe.

A WOMAN OF GREECE. This Greek lady is fully mistress of herself and might scarcely be at a loss to command others. Her wonderful costume bears a faint resemblance to those worn in the neighboring countries of Albania and Montenegro. She was photographed by Augustus Sherman.

A Pair of South Hollanders. Surely no pair could be more typically Dutch than this tiny brother and sister. Immigrants from the Netherlands already had three centuries of experience coming to America when these youngsters arrived at Ellis Island in the first decade of the 20th century. About 65,000 Dutch people passed through Ellis Island. This photograph was taken by Augustus Sherman.

East Africans on the Ellis Island Roof Garden. Thought to be natives of either Abyssinia or Somalia, these three immigrants were part of a large group, possibly an extended family. Augustus Sherman took this picture c. 1909.

A Gentleman from the Balkans. This immigrant, possibly from Albania or Montenegro, later found work with a pick and shovel at a miserable work site somewhere in America called Guinea Hill. The picture was taken *c.* 1908.

The Bavarian Miner. Wilhelm Schleich came from a small village in Bavaria. While Schleich was wearing his folk costume, which features a cameo photograph of King Ludwig II, Augustus Sherman took this 1906 photograph.

GYPSIES ON ELLIS ISLAND. This Gypsy (Romany) family emigrated from the Kingdom of Serbia and was photographed by Augustus Sherman on the roof garden. Although several thousand Gypsies passed through Ellis Island, some were detained as "professional beggars" and "vagrants." In 1911, many Gypsies were accused of these offenses and deported back to Argentina.

A YOUNG MAN OF ALGERIA. This Muslim Arab immigrant was one of many who passed through Ellis Island. The largest number of Arabs to immigrate during this period hailed from Syria, Lebanon, Egypt, Iraq, Algeria, and Morocco.

RUTHENIAN BEAUTY. Forming part of a steady stream of eastern European peasant migration, this woman was also photographed by Augustus Sherman. The Ruthenians were largely farmers and cattle herders.

RUSSIAN COSSACKS. This group photograph was taken by Sherman on the roof garden in 1907.

FOUR SARDINIAN BROTHERS, 1924. Like many other Mediterranean immigrants, the Soro brothers—Giomaria, Salvatore, Antonio, and Raffaele—came to America to earn money. Success allowed them to return to Sardinia and buy land. Until 1860, Sardinia had long been an independent kingdom, and it still has a strong identity thanks to its national language of Sardinian, which is as distinct a tongue as Italian or French.

A CHINESE IMMIGRANT. The Chinese division operated at Ellis Island from 1903 until 1954. Most of the work of its American inspectors and interpreters revolved around enforcing the Chinese Exclusion Act. In spite of this discriminatory law, certain loopholes allowed some people to be admitted. This Chinese woman was another subject of Augustus Sherman.

AN ARMENIAN REFUGEE, SEPTEMBER 30, 1920. Thousands of Armenian refugees fled persecutions in western Asia between 1890 and the 1920s. Absorbed and thoughtful, this Armenian woman seems to symbolize the plight of her nation. Well-known Armenians who passed through include abstract painter Arshile Gorky (Manouk Adoian) and restaurateur George Mardikian.

WLADEK ZBYSZKO. This Sherman portrait of the 250-pound world champion wrestler was taken at Ellis Island and dated May 24, 1918. From 1917 to 1918, Zbyszko was the world heavyweight champion and remained a contender in the 1920s. The Polish brothers Wladek (1891–1968) and Stanislaus Zbyszko (1878–1967) were among the most prominent European wrestlers of the 20th century. Their original surname was Cyganiewicz. In later years, they owned a pig farm in Missouri.

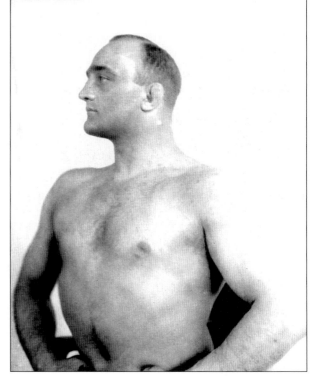

Four

LIFE ON ELLIS ISLAND AND IN AMERICA

AMERICA IN VIEW. This scene took place on the roof of the baggage and dormitory building, the station's largest detention building.

A CROWD OF DETAINEES. The dull, long, and uneasy days at Ellis Island were a trial for immigrants. Missionaries and immigrant aid workers made enduring these days somewhat easier. Ludmila K. Foxlee of the YWCA organized this event.

COLLECTING A FEW ALIENS. Immigrant men collecting relatives just off the boat was commonplace. Augustus Sherman took this photograph.

A Spot of Bread and Soup for Lunch. In this sketch, detainees are being served soup and bread on the roof garden. In this area, immigrants waited for a decision on their cases or the arrival of a relative. They might also get some exercise and take a peek at Manhattan and Jersey City through the fencing.

Mealtime in the Immigrant Dining Room. Women and children try to enjoy a meal at Ellis Island in the first decade of the 20th century.

JEWISH AID WORKERS AND IMMIGRANTS TOGETHER ABOARD THE *ELLIS ISLAND*. In 1905, the New York branch of the National Council of Jewish Women began aiding immigrants at Ellis Island. Sadie American (1862–1944), who sent aid workers to meet girls and women at the island, spearheaded this effort. In 1906, the council opened an office at the station. The Hebrew Immigrant Aid Society also had an important role at the station.

CECILIA GREENSTONE, "THE ANGEL OF ELLIS ISLAND." Born in Russia, Cecilia Greenstone (1887–1971) immigrated through Ellis Island in 1905 and was soon asked to join the National Council of Jewish Women by Sadie American. She was the council's preeminent agent at Ellis Island from 1906 through 1919. In 1914, she made a delicate mission to Europe for the Hebrew Immigrant Aid Society that ended curiously. This photograph was taken in 1918.

AN ITALIAN MOTHER WITH TWINS. One of the hardships of emigrating was caring for one's children, especially the very young. Fortunately, this mother looks fully capable of handling her own.

CHRISTIAN MISSIONARIES NEAR THE MAIN BUILDING. Missionaries usually cared for their own coreligionists. Here, we see Herr Aretz of the St. Raphaelsverein (German Catholics), Signor Carballo of the Italian Welfare League, Herr Kraut, and the Reverend Doering, a Protestant.

THE ITALIAN CATHOLIC VOICE OF ELLIS ISLAND. Fr. Gaspare Moretti (1880–1924), a Scalabrian missionary at Ellis Island and chaplain of St. Raphael's Home for Italian Immigrants, spoke these sad words in a 1910 Christmas address to excluded Italians: "I have spoken at Ellis Island before, but never [have] I felt so bad. There are so many detainees. You have found the door closed . . . your hope in the land of liberty shattered."

CHRISTMAS FOR DETAINED ALIENS. While religious services provided consolation, a grand Christmas tree, festivities, and presents were also offered to Christian detainees. During this 1905 Christmas, immigrants received fruit, sweets, and other presents. Standing next to Commissioner Watchorn (right) is a New York Bible Society missionary with his usual handful of tracts.

MADAME ERNESTINE SCHUMANN-HEINK PAYS A CALL. The great Austrian soprano gave a wonderful concert at Ellis Island during her visit to New York in 1909. She is seen here with members of her staff. Other entertainers who performed at the station included tenor Enrico Caruso, crooner Rudy Vallee, comedians Jimmy Durante and Bob Hope, and bandleader Lionel Hampton.

PRES. CIPRIANO CASTRO AT THE HEIGHT OF HIS POWER. One of the most controversial detainees in the history of Ellis Island was Cipriano Castro (1858–1924), former president of Venezuela (1899–1908). In December 1912, Castro sailed to New York, where he was unceremoniously taken to Ellis Island. A previous history of bad relations between him and Pres. Theodore Roosevelt was the cause. Castro was finally released on February 7, 1913. He died in Puerto Rico.

AUGUSTUS F. SHERMAN, PHOTOGRAPHER AND BUREAUCRAT. One of the leading figures at Ellis Island from *c.* 1900 to 1925 was longtime chief clerk Augustus Frederick Sherman (1865–1925). Remembered by the staff for his meticulousness, Sherman was also an outstanding photographer whose immigrant portraits seem to awaken the past. Born in Pennsylvania, Sherman settled in New York in 1889. At the time of his death, he was Commissioner Curran's confidential secretary.

WORLD WAR I DOUGHBOYS. These servicemen are enjoying themselves in the American Red Cross building *c.* 1920. The Red Cross House, as it was popularly called, was built in 1915 and pulled down in 1936. During World War I, thousands of wounded and sick soldiers and sailors received treatment in the Ellis Island hospital, and their stay was made more pleasant by programs sponsored by the Red Cross.

SCANDALOUS CONDITIONS. Following the end of World War I, there was a rush to emigrate to the United States. This picture shows how poorly prepared the station was in coping with this influx under Commissioner Frederick Wallis in 1921.

LUDMILA KUCHAR FOXLEE, PORT WORKER. An energetic social worker, Ludmila Foxlee (1885–1971) was a native of Bohemia who had emigrated to the United States with her family in the 1890s. Because of her linguistic talent—she knew several languages as well as her native Czech—she was appointed YWCA port work at Ellis Island in 1920 and continued working there until 1937. She was fascinated by folk costumes and assimilation.

AUSTRIANS AT THE RAILWAY DOCK. Ludmila Foxlee of the YWCA helped this immigrant family. Three family members have Baltimore and Ohio Railroad and Central Railroad train tags attached to their clothing to indicate they that are waiting for the ferry to Jersey City to continue their inland journey. They are standing in front of the first Ellis Island greenhouse.

A SOUTHERN EUROPEAN THREESOME. These brothers can scarcely keep still, but the artful Augustus Sherman has managed to capture something of their elusive charm in this portrait.

Seven Russians. In July 1923, these Russians arrived at Ellis Island and were aided in their troubles by YWCA port worker Ludmila Foxlee.

The Waiting Game. This motley group lounging on the grass gives a hint of what was in store for immigrants at Ellis Island during this period—infinite boredom.

TURN IT OFF COMPLETELY WHILE WE FIX IT RIGHT! This cartoon refers to the Johnson-Reed Act of 1924, which severely reduced the free flow of immigrants into the United States by imposing strict annual quotas for most of the countries of origin.

AN ORPHAN IN THE SAND. Like many Armenians, Tourvanda Ahigian escaped from the massacres of her nation in 1915–1920. After years in an Egyptian orphanage, she emigrated to America and found herself detained at Ellis Island for two months in 1928. Eventually settling in Michigan, she married and became known as Victoria Haroutunian. In the 1990s, she returned to Ellis Island with her daughter Virginia Haroutunian and shared long hidden memories of horror and war.

ALIENS IN WAITING. There is a hint of tension as these immigrants sit in one of the many waiting rooms at Ellis Island in the 1930s. To be on Ellis Island in these years was to be in a perpetual state of uncertainty, for deportations were high. Notable immigrants entering during this transitional period were novelist Ayn Rand (1926), Yiddish singer Sidor Belarsky (1930), and the Trapp Family Singers (1938).

THE IMMIGRANT AID CORRIDOR. This photograph shows the location of immigrant aid societies in the main building on April 21, 1933. Near the woman on the left is the nameplate of the city mission society. In December 1932, just a few months before this picture was taken, Eleanor Roosevelt, the wife of New York's governor, Franklin D. Roosevelt, visited the station.

COMMISSIONER EDWARD CORSI. In 1931, President Hoover appointed this Italian immigrant to head Ellis Island. Corsi, who had immigrated through the station in 1907, had strong feelings about his service at Ellis Island and the conditions he found there. After leaving office in 1934, he wrote a book about them. A prominent social worker, Edward Corsi (1896–1965), later served in the Eisenhower administration. In 1965, he endorsed the selection of Ellis Island as a national monument.

FAREWELL TO AMERICA—FOR NOW. These Italian deportees appear to have swallowed their rejection at Ellis Island with aplomb. Deporting squad officers escorted deportees to their steamships and stood watching on the pier until the vessel was cleared for sailing.

A Hint of Reality. This 1930s-era Deporting Division sign is one of the many artifacts found at Ellis Island long after its abandonment. The sign is made of wood, and its gold-painted lettering is edged in black.

Life in a New York City Tenement. Immigrants struggled to make a livelihood in America. This sketch shows how children were employed illegally as tobacco strippers in their tenement flat on the East Side of Manhattan.

LITTLE ITALY'S MULBERRY STREET. This classic scene of America's greatest Italian community shows the horse-drawn wagons, the vegetable and fruit peddlers with their wares, the crowd itself, the shops, and the tenement buildings.

AN ITALIAN IMMIGRANT FAMILY AT MEALTIME. Immigrants, especially the Italians, brought to the New World a rich culinary tradition that was long available only in ethnic communities. Today, immigrant cuisine can be had most anywhere.

THE IMPACT OF IMMIGRATION ON AMERICAN POPULAR CULTURE. Claire Rochester, the famous vaudeville artiste, recorded this song c. 1920. Other vaudevillians who sang comic or romantic songs about immigrants included Nora Bayes, "Has Anybody Here Seen Kelly?"; Jack Norworth, "Rosa Rosetta"; and Elsie Janis, "When Angelo Plays His Cello." The most popular immigrant nationalities in ethnic recordings and on the vaudeville stage were the Irish, Germans, Jews, Chinese, and Italians.

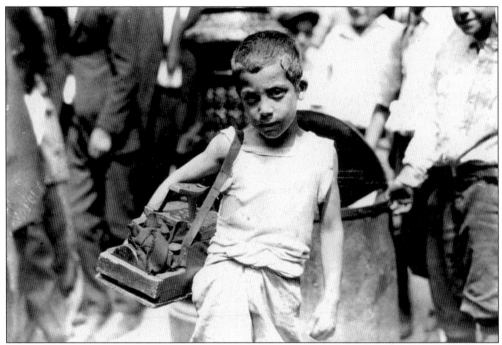

A SHOESHINE BOY. Cities like New York, Boston, Philadelphia, Chicago, and San Francisco swarmed with immigrant children providing this kind of service. Other children sold shoestrings, matches, newspapers, or trinkets.

FACTORY WORK. The Industrial Revolution provided monotonous but fairly steady work for hundreds of thousands of immigrants during the 19th and 20th centuries. However, the hours were long and the pay was often a pittance.

CITIZENSHIP FOR SOLDIERS. Military service during wartime was always tempting because the reward was almost instant citizenship. These immigrant inductees during World War I take the oath of allegiance to the United States during their naturalization ceremony in 1918. The Civil War and World War II also attracted huge numbers of immigrants.

NEW AMERICANS. Peacetime naturalizations also remained steady. Here, male aliens become American citizens. Women were often slower in applying for U.S. citizenship.

IMMIGRANT CHILDREN AT PLAY. This late-1920s picture shows the typical life of immigrant children in a tenement neighborhood in New York City.

THE PORTUGUESE FISHERMEN. Some immigrants continued their old line of work in America. These Portuguese fishermen continued their lifestyle in their new home in Cape Cod, Massachusetts, while others did the same in New Bedford, Massachusetts, as well as farther afield in Newark, New Jersey, and San Diego, California.

Five
THE FINAL YEARS

THE LANING MURAL AT ELLIS ISLAND. Seen here is a portion of the giant mural that was painted at Ellis Island by the well-known artist Edward Laning (1906–1981) from 1936 to 1938. The mural, which was sponsored by the Work Projects Administration, celebrates the role of immigrants in the building up of America. It was removed from the island in 1964 and reinstalled in a federal courthouse in Brooklyn.

ELLIS ISLAND. This 1936 B-movie was a rousing adventure about two inspectors of the deporting squad who are caught up in an intriguing web of mobsters, deportees, and a missing $1 million. It starred Donald Cook, Johnny Arthur, Peggy Shannon, Jack LaRue, and Joyce Compton. Two years later, another Ellis Island film, *Gateway*, was released with a cast headed by Don Ameche, Arleen Whelan, and Binnie Barnes.

BETWEEN ISLANDS TWO AND THREE. Here, we get a view of the solarium and, behind it, the recreation building. Immigrants recovering from ill health take in the fresh air here. This stands between the general immigrant hospital buildings (right) and the contagious disease wards (left), neither of which can be seen in this picture.

THE ELLIS ISLAND SCHOOLROOM. Extended family detentions made life dull for children until the Ellis Island schoolroom was started. This *c.* 1937 photograph shows the children reading and playing; a few are watching the camera.

A BUREAUCRAT FOR ALL SEASONS. Byron H. Uhl (1873–1944), perhaps the longest serving employee at Ellis Island, rose from stenographer in 1892 to district director (commissioner) by 1940. A few of his most famous cases include the successful deportation of anarchist Emma Goldman (1919), the failed attempts to exclude former Venezuelan dictator Cipriano Castro, British suffragette Emmeline Pankhurst (1913), and Vera, Countess of Cathcart, an English noblewoman (1926).

Uhl Will Mark Half-Century On Ellis Island

To Mark 50 Years' Service

Immigration Official, 68, Yearns for Country Cottage With Broad Green Vistas

Bryon H. Uhl, district director of he Immigration and Naturalization Service, who on Thursday will cele- rate his fiftieth anniversary on Ellis Island, looked out of the win- low of his water-bound office yes- erday and admitted to a longing o settle down for the rest of his ears in a little land-locked house n the country.

Just how soon he will retire he vouldn't say, but he ventured that it will be sooner than a lot of people hink."

Mr. Uhl has no particular aver- sion to large expanses of water, but he thinks that after fifty years of working on an island, green vistas might offer a welcome change.

A. F. Sozio

Byron H. Uhl

ENEMY ALIENS. In the 1940s, the registry room was renamed Passenger Hall and used as a day room for German enemy alien families. From December 1941 through 1947, thousands of Germans, Italians, and Japanese were arrested as suspects by the Federal Bureau of Investigation and taken to Ellis Island. Hundreds more included Germans from Latin America. Italian opera singer Ezio Pinza was held for several weeks in 1942 on suspicions that he might be a Fascist spy.

GERMAN REFUGEES IN EUROPE, 1945. Conditions in Europe were desperate for millions of people at the close of World War II. Refugees and displaced persons swarmed over continental Europe after the fall of the Third Reich. Many later emigrated to the United States aboard army transport ships and passed through Ellis Island.

BRITISH EVACUEES GREET THE GODDESS OF LIBERTY. During World War II, thousands of British schoolchildren were evacuated from their homeland to safety in Canada and the United States. These English children entering New York harbor in 1942 are hailing the Statue of Liberty as their ship enters the harbor.

THE COAST GUARD POST EXCHANGE OPENS ON ELLIS ISLAND. Coast Guardsman Ralph Hornberger (right) is pictured here with his friend young Mr. Mathieu (left) at the opening of the latter's exchange. The picture shows the till on the right and various goods, including candies, chewing gum, and cigarettes, on the left. The Coast Guard trained and sheltered over 60,000 men there from 1939 to 1946 and from 1951 to 1954.

MONEY FOR THE AMERICAN MUSEUM OF IMMIGRATION. Fundraising for the American Museum of Immigration (AMI) began in 1952. Here, park service historian Thomas M. Pitkin (1901–1988) accepts a check for the museum from a North Carolina high school on October 28, 1956. The museum was built on Liberty Island and was dedicated by President Nixon in 1972. However, the restoration of Ellis Island led to the museum's closing in 1991.

ELLIS ISLAND, C. 1957. In the foreground are Ellis Island and the old Jersey City railroad docks. Farther off is Bedloe's Island and the Statue of Liberty. Even farther away are the boroughs of Staten Island (right) and Brooklyn (left).

Six

A Glimpse at the Hall of Fame

EDWARD G. ROBINSON. One of Hollywood's greatest actors, Edward G. Robinson (1893–1973) was born in Romania. His original name was Emmanuel Goldenberg. Like many European immigrants, he thought he was entering *Kessel garten* (Castle Garden). Later on, when he learned it was really Ellis Island, he said, "At Ellis Island I was born again; life began for me when I was ten years old."

ARTHUR TRACY. From the vaudeville stage of the 1920s emerged Arthur Tracy (1899–1997), "the Street Singer," whose hauntingly beautiful voice won him international acclaim on stage, screen, and radio. Born in a *shtetl* in Kemenets-Podolsk, Russia, as Abba Trasskavutsky, he and his family arrived at Ellis Island in 1906. They settled in Philadelphia and changed their name to Tracy. Arthur performed in the Yiddish theater in 1917 but soon switched to the vaudeville stage. He made his greatest mark in radio, where he could reach millions of listeners. Tracy always sang with elegance and feeling. His vocal powers were especially well displayed when singing such ballads as "East of the Sun," "Pennies from Heaven," "Trees," "September in the Rain," "The Way You Look Tonight," "(In My) Solitude," "Red Sails in the Sunset," "The Whistling Waltz," and "When I Grow Old to Dream." His theme song, "Marta," which he sang while playing the accordion, was instantly recognizable to millions in the golden age of radio. Among his films are *The Street Singer*, *Command Performance*, and *Follow Your Star*.

KNUTE ROCKNE. An icon of American football, Knute Rockne (1888–1931) was born in Voss, Norway. Little Knut Rokne and his mother passed through Ellis Island in 1893 and joined his father, Lars, in Chicago. Knute attended Notre Dame University and stayed on as its football coach for the rest of his life. His fame rests on his perfection of the forward pass and the triumphs of the Fighting Irish.

WARNER OLAND. The one and only Charlie Chan of the movies, Warner Oland (1880–1938) left Sweden in 1894 as Jonah Werner Ohlund and settled in Connecticut. After years as a stage actor, he gained success on the silent screen, which led to stardom in talkies. His film credits include *Chinatown Nights*, *The Mysterious Fu Manchu*, *Charlie Chan Carries On*, *The Painted Veil*, and *Charlie Chan in Egypt*. He died in Sweden.

FATHER FLANAGAN. Edward Joseph Flanagan (1886–1948) left his native Ireland in 1904 to study for the priesthood. He sailed to America aboard the *Celtic*. Although he had no trouble getting through Ellis Island, it took time before he was accepted at a seminary. As a priest in Omaha, Nebraska, he founded Boys Town in 1917, and his efforts as a reformer earned him acclaim. He died in Berlin, Germany.

PAULINE NEWMAN. An important official of the International Ladies Garment Workers Union for over 60 years, Pauline Newman was born in Lithuania and was processed at Ellis Island in 1901. After working for several years at the Triangle Shirtwaist factory, she became a union organizer. She also advocated women's suffrage. She died in 1986.

FRANK CAPRA (LEFT). Hollywood would have never been quite the same without the delightful films made by director Frank Capra (1897–1991), born in Sicily. His family arrived at Ellis Island in 1903 and then took a train to Los Angeles. Capra's classic films include *It Happened One Night* (which starred Clark Gable and Claudette Colbert), *You Can't Take It With You, Mr. Deeds Goes to Town*, and *It's a Wonderful Life*.

CLAUDETTE COLBERT. Born in Paris, France, young Lily Claudette Chauchoin came to America with her mother in 1906. As unescorted females, they were detained at Ellis Island until her father, Georges, came to claim them. Claudette Colbert (1903–1996) became one of Hollywood's top box office attractions. Her greatest films include *Cleopatra, The Misleading Lady, I Cover the Waterfront, Imitation of Life, Tovarich, Drums along the Mohawk*, and *Since You Went Away*.

103

JOHNNY WEISSMULLER. The 1920s Olympic gold medalist Johnny Weissmuller (1904–1984) was born in Freidorf, Austria-Hungary, as Peter Jonas Weissmuller. His family arrived at Ellis Island in 1906 and settled in Chicago. Beginning in 1932, the swimming champion became the greatest screen Tarzan ever, appearing in 12 Tarzan films, including *Tarzan the Ape Man*, *Tarzan's Secret Treasure*, and *Tarzan Triumphs*. From 1933 to 1938, Weissmuller had a tempestuous marriage to Mexican actress Lupe Velez.

BOB HOPE. The legendary comedian was born Leslie Hope in Eltham, England, in 1903 and immigrated through Ellis Island with his family in 1908. They settled in Ohio. Hope went into vaudeville in the 1920s and achieved fame on Broadway by 1933. From there, he went on to become one of Hollywood's biggest stars, conquering motion pictures, radio, and television. For decades, he entertained America's troops abroad.

ERICH VON STROHEIM. Erich Oswald Stroheim (1885–1957) left Austria a commoner in 1909; it was only after leaving Ellis Island that he appended the aristocratic "von" to his name. He was acclaimed "the Man You Love to Hate;" his fame rests on the dazzlingly decadent films he made in the 1920s and his eccentric screen performances. His films include *The Devil's Pass Key*, *Foolish Wives*, *Greed*, *Grand Illusion*, and *Sunset Boulevard*. He died in France.

XAVIER CUGAT (RIGHT). The future king of rumba music sailed from Havana to Ellis Island with his uncle in 1915. Cugat (1900–1990) was born in Barcelona, Spain, but was taken to Cuba when he was very young. For years, his orchestra broadcasted live from the Waldorf Hotel with such popular songs as "My Shawl," "El Sombrero de Gaspar," and "Silencio." His first wife, Mexican singer Carmen Castillo, also immigrated through Ellis Island.

IGOR SIKORSKY. The man who built the first successful helicopter (1939), Igor Sikorsky (1889–1971) was already a leading aeronautical engineer when he was forced to flee Russia after the fall of the tsar. Sikorsky arrived nearly penniless at Ellis Island in 1919. In Connecticut, he set up the Sikorsky Aircraft Corporation and continued his pioneering work in aviation. His helicopter, the VS-300, won him worldwide acclaim.

MISCHA AUER (LEFT). One of the zaniest actors of the golden age of Hollywood, Mischa Ounskowsky escaped from Russia in 1920, joining other refugees in New York. His success at stage acting quickly led to a cinematic career in which he dazzled audiences in films such as *My Man Godfrey*, *You Can't Take It With You*, *Destry Rides Again*, and *Brewster's Millions*. Mischa Auer (1905–1967) eventually returned to Europe.

BELA LUGOSI. Screen legend Bela Lugosi (1882–1956) fled his native Hungary for political reasons. By 1920, he had entered the United States illegally by jumping ship in New Orleans. In New York, he eventually surrendered to immigration authorities at Ellis Island and was admitted by inspector John Richardson on March 23, 1921. For political reasons, he claimed to be Romanian. Among his greatest films are *Dracula, White Zombie,* and *The Raven.*

RONALD COLMAN. Following the end of the World War I, Ronald Colman (1891–1958), an unemployed shipping clerk, passed through Ellis Island in 1920 and settled in New York. At a crossroads, he wanted to become a professional actor. Success on the stage soon led to film stardom in Hollywood. His credits include *The Devil to Pay, Lost Horizon, The Prisoner of Zenda, A Double Life,* and *Champagne for Caesar.*

GEORGE BRENT. After his activity in the Irish Republican Army made things uncomfortable, Irish-born George Brendan Nolan (1904–1979) came to the United States in 1922. He changed his name to George Brent and went on the American stage. By 1931, he was in Hollywood and went on to enjoy a long career as a leading man. His best films include *The Painted Veil, Jezebel, Dark Victory, The Fighting 69th,* and *Illegal Entry.*

RICARDO CORTEZ. Cashing in on the Valentino craze of the 1920s, Jacob Kranz became a Latin lover and for a time quite a success. An Austrian Jew, he passed through Ellis Island in 1921. The best film in which Ricardo Cortez (1899–1977) starred in was *The Torrent,* opposite Greta Garbo. His others films include *Argentine Love, The Spaniard, Volcano, Inside Story,* and *City of Chance.*

JIDDU KRISHNAMURTI. The revered Indian spiritual teacher and philosopher Krishnamurti (1895–1986) came to the United States for a visit in 1922. He eventually settled permanently in Ojai, California, lecturing and writing such books as *This Matter of Culture* and *You Are the World*.

PAULINE TRIGÈRE. Pauline Trigère (1908–2001) emigrated from France in 1937 with virtually nothing. In 1942, she opened her fashion design business, and from the 1950s through the 1970s, she was a leading New York designer of elegant clothing and accessories. Her handbags were especially famous.

CHARLES TRENET. The great French singer Charles Trenet (1913–2001) never intended to immigrate to the United States. His Ellis Island experience resulted in his running afoul of the law. In 1948, he sailed to New York for theatrical engagements, but on his arrival, he was quickly detained at Ellis Island on charges of homosexuality. Release came after 26 days in detention. He had similar difficulties in France.

ARTHUR TRACY RETURNS TO ELLIS ISLAND. Arthur Tracy, "the Street Singer," is shown on February 15, 1995, when he returned to Ellis Island for an oral history interview. It was his first visit to the island since 1906. He received the Ellis Island Medal of Honor in 1996.

Seven

NEGLECT AND PRESERVATION

NEW YORK HARBOR. This aerial shot was taken on May 2, 1956, at 12:15 p.m., at an altitude of 300 feet. In the foreground is the Statue of Liberty, and in the distance are Manhattan, a passing steamship, and a barge and tugboat. On the right is the Brooklyn Bridge.

THE GREAT HALL ABANDONED. This photograph was taken in 1956, a couple of years after Ellis Island was closed by the Immigration and Naturalization Service and declared surplus government property. Attempts to give the island to another federal agency or sell it to private owners failed.

A NATIONAL MONUMENT. On May 11, 1965, President Johnson declared Ellis Island a national monument, citing the fact that noteworthy immigrants such as Irving Berlin, David Sarnoff, Spyros Skouras, and Vice Pres. Hubert Humphrey's Norwegian mother had entered the country through the facility. He made it a part of the Statue of Liberty National Monument and the responsibility of the National Park Service. He is pictured here signing the new immigration bill into law on Liberty Island in 1965.

THE GREAT HALL IN DECAY. In spite of the island's national monument status, the buildings continued on a downward spiral of decay. In addition, vandals came to the island to steal the large quantity of furniture and other items that had been left behind.

THE RAILROAD TICKET OFFICE. Seen here is an agent's booth in the railroad ticket office, also known as the railroad room.

THE COAST GUARD RECREATION ROOM. This old Kruger piano is still gathering dust on the second floor of the dormitory and baggage building. Although not pictured, an enormous old German safe stands nearby.

A COAST GUARD TRAINING DIAGRAM. This is a telling remnant of the training program set up at Ellis Island for the thousands of young coastguardsmen during World War II.

A STAIRCASE IN THE BAGGAGE AND DORMITORY BUILDING. The main detention building at Ellis Island, this is where the Jewish anarchist Emma Goldman, the Italian gangster Lucky Luciano, and the Trinidadian Socialist C.L.R. James were held before their deportations. Numerous Nazi and Fascist enemy aliens and a host of others were also detained here. The building is badly neglected.

THE FERRYBOAT *ELLIS ISLAND*. Neglect of the *Ellis Island* caused it to sink in a storm in August 1968. Now, only its hull is left in the slip. Launched in March 1904, the *Ellis Island* held 1,000 passengers and logged over a million miles as it went back and forth across New York harbor. It served the immigration staff and ferried released aliens to Manhattan.

THE ELLIS ISLAND OPENING CEREMONY. In 1976, thanks to the efforts of Peter Sammartino and his Ellis Island Restoration Commission, the island was partially cleaned up and opened for limited visitation. This crowd of concerned citizens demonstrated the importance of Ellis Island to the nation. It was closed again in 1984 for the restoration.

THE RESTORATION OF THE GREAT HALL. It was not until Ronald Reagan became president in 1981 that a serious effort to restore the abandoned station was begun. This photograph shows the tremendous scaffolding that was set up in the registry room to aid restorers and workers.

A Bridge to New Jersey. This service bridge was built in 1984 to allow supplies to be brought to Ellis Island during the restoration. It will eventually be removed.

A Detention Building Stairway. Pictured here is another of the many staircases in the three-storied baggage and dormitory building. Note the restraining fence secured to the balustrade. It was designed to prevent aliens from escaping. This picture was taken in 1996.

THE KITCHEN BAKERY. This 1996 picture shows the old bakery room in the kitchen facility of the baggage and dormitory building.

A SWASTIKA. This graffiti is inscribed on the walls of a detention cell in the baggage and dormitory building. From 1941 to 1947, German enemy aliens were held at Ellis Island as prisoners of war. Quite a number of them were active members of the Nazi movement.

A National Park Service Brochure. The author wrote the text of this 1997 brochure explaining the role Ellis Island played during World War II.

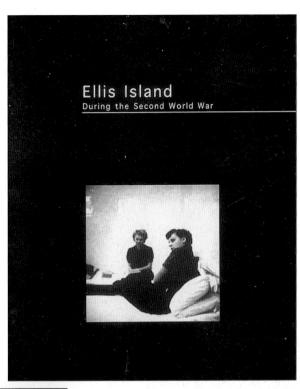

Ellis Island
During the Second World War

A View of the Statue of Liberty from Ellis Island. The confinement of aliens at Ellis Island did not prevent them from getting a superb view of the Statue of Liberty, America's preeminent icon of freedom.

A ROOFTOP VISIT. This photograph of the author was taken on the rooftop of the psychopathic ward on Island Two in March 1999. The abandoned hospital buildings on Islands Two and Three have recently been stabilized, and an organization called Save Ellis Island! is raising funds to restore them completely.

A MATTRESS STEAM CLEANER. This machine, located in the contagious disease hospital on Island Three, was important in preventing the spread of disease.

THE AUTOPSY ROOM. These refrigerated units held corpses. Autopsies were also performed in this room in the contagious disease hospital on Island Three. Between 3,000 and 4,000 immigrants died on Ellis Island. Burials were off-site.

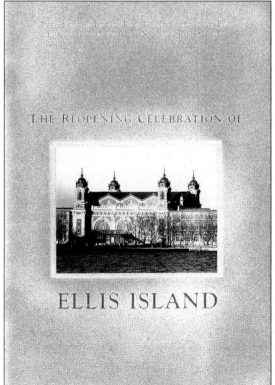

THE REOPENING CELEBRATION OF

ELLIS ISLAND

THE 1990 REOPENING OF ELLIS ISLAND. The restoration of the main building was finally achieved with the dedication of the Ellis Island Immigration Museum in September 1990. The Statue of Liberty-Ellis Island Foundation raised hundreds of millions of dollars to do it. The new museum was formally dedicated by Vice Pres. J. Danforth Quayle, assisted by Lee A. Iacocca, chairman of the foundation.

THE MAIN ENTRANCE TO THE ELLIS ISLAND IMMIGRATION MUSEUM. The newly restored main building has a steel-and-glass canopy added during the restoration. In a modest way, it replaces the original canopy that adorned the entrance from 1903 until 1931. The sign and plinth were added in 1999.

TOURISTS AT ELLIS ISLAND. Since its reopening as a museum in 1990, more than 20 million visitors have paid a call at Ellis Island.

A STAIRCASE VIEW OF THE REGISTRY ROOM. The restored Great Hall appears as it did in 1918, with the original chandeliers, wooden benches, and Catalan tiles. The tiles for the vaulted ceiling and the floor were designed and installed by the firm of Rafael Guastavino.

THE REGISTRY ROOM. This more complete view of the Great Hall shows the original benches on display as well as the reproduced inspectors' desks near the stairs of separation at the end of the hall. In keeping with the 1918 theme, the flags have only 48 stars.

A RANGER GUIDED TOUR. The National Park Service, which administers the museum, provides various interpretive programs at Ellis Island. Here, park ranger Carol Kelly explains Ellis Island's history to a receptive audience. Visitors can also obtain immigration records in the American Family Immigration History Center, which was opened by the Statue of Liberty-Ellis Island Foundation in April 2001.

THE *SILENT VOICES* EXHIBIT GALLERY. This exhibit evokes the years of Ellis Island's neglect by showing the many furnishings left to decay.

ELLIS ISLAND AND THE AMERICAN IMMIGRANT WALL OF HONOR. The stainless-steel American Immigrant Wall of Honor was built in two phases, the first in 1993 and the second in 1998–1999. Sponsored by the Statue of Liberty-Ellis Island Foundation, it has more than 600,000 names of immigrants of all periods of American history inscribed on it. It replaced a temporary copper wall of honor that had been installed in 1989–1990 on a portion of the sea wall near the flagpole.

ACKNOWLEDGMENTS

For many years, I have been fortunate in working with a fine group of colleagues at the Statue of Liberty and Ellis Island. I am grateful for their unfailing encouragement and kindness in all of my endeavors at the monument and museum. In particular, I would like to thank Jeffrey S. Dosik, Diana Pardue, Eric Byron, Janet Levine, Kevin Daley, Cynthia Garrett, George Tselos, Sydney Onikul, Frank Mills, Ken Glasgow, Richard D. Holmes, Don Fiorino, Judith Giuriceo, Paul Roper, Geraldine Santoro, Nora Mulrooney, Doug Tarr, Michael Conklin, Steve Thornton, Brian Feeney, Peter Stolz, Peg Zitko, Sgt. Charles Guddemi of the park police, David Diakow, Katharine Daley, and my friends who work on the Statue of Liberty-Ellis Island ferry boats, especially Luciano Terkovich.

I would also like to thank our park's volunteers, especially Charles "Chick" Lemonick, David Cassells, Marcus Smith, John Kiyusu, Mary Fleming, North and Jesse Peterson, Javier Agramonte, and the late Richard Kwiatkowski. The research and friendship of historians Marian L. Smith of the U.S. Bureau of Citizenship and Immigration Services, Peter Mesenhoeller of Germany (who has generously shared his research on Augustus Sherman), Brian G. Andersson of the New York City Municipal Archives, Robert Stein of the City University of New York, and Robert Morris and John Celardo of the National Archives, have also been invaluable. In addition, I appreciate the help and encouragement of my friends Loretto D. Szucs, Philip Wilner, Lorie Conway, Joseph Michalak, Kevin Sherlock, Louise Muse, Rosemary Gelshenen, John Devanny, Isabel Belarsky, Tom Bernardin, Brian Ockram, and the late vaudeville and radio star Arthur Tracy, known as "the Street Singer." Because I have long admired the books made by Arcadia Publishing, I must thank editors Susan E. Jaggard and Pamela O'Neil, as well as graphic designer Brendan Cornwell, for letting me work on this book with them.

The pictures in this volume are largely drawn from the collections of the National Park Service, the Library of Congress, the National Archives, and the U.S. Bureau of Immigration. Those from other collections are as follows: Ellis Island Dining Room (p. 110), New York Public Library; Rev. Fr. Gaspare Moretti (p. 63), Dr. Emelise Aleandri's *Little Italy*; Cipriano Castro (p. 79), Corbis/Bettman; and Mulberry Street (p. 88), Museum of the City of New York. From the author's collection came the *Paris* (p. 28); *Ellis Island,* (p. 94); *The Street Singer's Radio Song Book,* (p. 100); Oland (p. 101); Newman (p. 102); Weissmuller (p. 104); Von Stroheim and Cugat (p. 105); Auer (p. 106); Colman (p. 107); Cortez (p. 108); Trenet (p. 110); a World War II brochure and view of the Statue of Liberty (p. 119); the author on the roof (p. 120); the autopsy room and Ellis reopening brochure (p. 121); and *Silent Voices* (p. 124).

INDEX